Lemn Sissay is a poet, playwright and broadcaster. He contributes regularly to BBC radio. He reads his poetry on stages worldwide. From Arizona to Zimbabwe, his award-winning play, *Something Dark*, toured to packed audiences and rave reviews. Recent residencies include California State University and he is currently artist in residence at the award-winning Southbank Centre. His poems have become landmarks on the streets and walls of Manchester, England and are featured in sculpture in the City of London. His work has been the inspiration for a concerto at the BBC Proms, performed at London's Royal Albert Hall, and he appears on the multi-award-winning Leftfield album *Leftism*. He is patron of the Letterbox Club, a Booktrust initiative to get books to young people in care, and he is education ambassador for the Arvon Foundation for writing. He was born in Lancashire of Ethiopian and Eritrean heritage.

www.lemnsissay.com

Also by Lemn Sissay

Poetry
Tender Fingers in a Clenched Fist
Rebel without Applause
Morning Breaks in the Elevator
The Fire People (edited by Lemn Sissay)
The Emperor's Watchmaker

Plays
Something Dark
(available in *Hidden Gems*, edited by Deirdre Osborne)

For Sarah

LISTENER

Wishes

LEMN SISSAY

[signature] 2019

CANONGATE
Edinburgh · London

First published in Great Britain in 2008 by
Canongate Books Ltd, 14 High Street,
Edinburgh EH1 1TE

British Library Cataloguing-in-Publication Data
A catalogue record for this book is available on request from the British Library.

ISBN 978 1 84195 895 8

Typeset by Cluny Sheeler

Printed and bound in Great Britain by Clays Ltd, Elcograf S.p.A.

www.canongate.tv

'To go step by step we begin with the personal pronouns and the verb "to be".'

Semere Woldegabir, *Amharic for Foreigners*

'If, as Marx said, religion is the opiate of the people, then nationalism is the crack cocaine.'

Gaiem Kibreab, Birkbeck College, May 2008

CONTENTS

LET THERE BE PEACE

Let there be peace
So frowns fly away like albatross
And skeletons foxtrot from cupboards;
So war correspondents become travel show presenters
And magpies bring back lost property,
Children, engagement rings, broken things.

Let there be peace
So storms can go out to sea to be
Angry and return to me calm;
So the broken can rise and dance in the hospitals.
Let the aged Ethiopian man in the grey block of flats
Peer through his window and see Addis before him
So his thrilled outstretched arms become frames
For his dreams.

Let there be peace.
Let tears evaporate to form clouds, cleanse themselves
And fall into reservoirs of drinking water.
Let harsh memories burst into fireworks that melt
In the dark pupils of a child's eyes
And disappear like shoals of darting silver fish.
And let the waves reach the shore with a
Shhhhhhhhhh shhhhhhhhh shhhhhhhhhhh.

RAIN

w f t n w t r w r i c

h a c r e u

e l a h a t

n l h i t 's n

t l e e i h i

h k s u i n t i

s n m n n b a

e t p k h n

r h o e t h f o e

e f h a o

a m r n a w

i y b e f m w

a u t l s a

n t l a

s n y

THE ACTOR'S VOICE

This is a celebration of sound,
Of words said after the phone's put down,
After the door's shut at the editor's cut –
Of thoughts held after the word 'but . . .'
This is the sound. The actor's sound.
Of inflections after the flick of ash,
Before the crash, before the whiplash;
Of thoughts collecting before they arrive,
Of the deep breath before the dive.
This is the sound,
Of tender fingers in a clenched fist,
Of the wind carrying an invisible kiss,
Of a secret unfolding wish,
Before the candle blows like a lisp.

This is a celebration of sound,
Of words said after the phone's put down,
After the door's shut at the editor's cut –
Thoughts said after the word 'but . . .'
Thoughts caught between the lines –
The reading sounds of needing minds.
This is the sound of beneath the laugh,
Beneath the draft, beneath the craft –
The space between the paragraphs,

The pause between the polygraph,
The actor acting out of her skin,
The sound of shedding sins.

The sound of spirit, the sound of soul,
The sound of heat, the sound of old
Dreams fading, reawakening time;
Of hope breaking the mould of mind,
Of the beat before the hands clap,
The click, the clack, the trip, the trap;
The sound before a dropping latch,
The sound of looking back – the 22nd catch.

This is a celebration of sound,
Words said after the phone's put down,
After the door's shut at the editor's cut –
Thoughts held after the word 'but . . .';
This is the sound before death;
In the beginning it wasn't the word,
It was breath.

PATTERNS

2. Have
7. Have
10. Innocence
5. Pattern
8. Lost
1. You
4. A
9. Your
3. Found
6. You

MOVING TARGET

As long as they think they can push you
Around with unwritten laws
Saying which kind of car you can drive,
Which woman you can date,
Which occupation you can take,
Or which street you can live in,
You are not safe.

As long as they think they can push you
Around with unwritten laws
Saying how your name should be shortened,
Which food you should eat,
Which way you should wear your hair,
Which house you should live in,
Which language you should use,
You are not safe.
As long as they think you are a target
They will take aim.

As long as they think they can push you
Around with unwritten laws
About which country you should live in,
Which smell you should prefer,
Which restaurants you should eat in,
Which places you should go to at night,

Which cricket team you should support,
Or which route your child or friend should
         take to school,
You are not safe.

As long as they think you are a target
They will take aim.
Do not get used to these thoughts,
Do not engage with them,
They will devour you.
Do not wear them or grow with them,
Do not challenge them or walk in them,
Do not counter them.

LAYING THE TABLE

We should prepare for arguments,
Lay down the tablecloth
And silently place the cutlery
In exactly the right place.

We should serve each other's food
And eat with our hands,
Pick at the chicken,
Maul the potatoes.

We should then wipe our mouths
With the tablecloth and begin.

PERFECT

You are so perfect
When you kick them the leaves flit to the trees,
Look back to you and applaud.
You are so perfect
Branches part in forests to share sun's shine,
Squirrels watch you between acorns,
Foxes wake.

You are so perfect
Your winter coat buttons itself and hugs your heart,
Library books unfurl on tables, stretch
And wait for you to walk past.
Fast winter wind daren't touch you
But can't help brush your hair.

You are so perfect
Rivers have built their own bridges,
Knowing that one day you'll walk across them –
Just to catch your reflection they left a pile of stones for
          you to throw.
And the waves carry each stone to the bed, count them,
Look up at you and applaud.

You are so perfect
Traffic lights time themselves days before you arrive

So your stride won't be broken and the cars can rest
And the world can stop.
A table outside the café lays itself to the waiter's amazement
Knowing that a man will stop for a coffee,
Knowing that you will walk past at 3.30 p.m.,
And he'd been waiting for you all of his life too.

GAMBIAN HOLIDAY MAKER

I

Want

You

To

Know

How

Stupid

You

Sound

When

You

Talk

To

Us

Like

This.

LISTENER

And if you were the evaporating tears
Then I would be the developing cloud.
There, the sound of rain,
The sound of the between-us-sea,
The shingle shore gently fills our footsteps.
I have searched for you my entire life.
We have stood on opposite shores
Listening to under-sea wails.
No translations as yet, but this.

I lie upon the earth-floor
As a lion might in deep dusk-sun.
Here I hear all the footsteps of the world
Reverberate in the beneath-me-rocks,
Trying to find your first person singular steps,
Trying to find a sentence in a history,
But the needle glints in the golden haystack
Of dawn at the same time a strike of sunlight
Lances its eye. The world is smaller,
The larger my knowledge – still.

Standing, I hear the sun rise,
Not the birds of morning nor the cock crowing.
The cars coughing the footsteps of early workers
Muffled in the red dust trudging through sleepless mystery
But I hear the actual sun rising.

And as a sea can turn to dust before the eyes
I hear you through the sand storm – *the needle!*
Slow running from the red terror
Arms wide to protect yourself or welcome me,
Feet dragging through sand and globules of blood
Burning in the heatwave wiping hot sand from your face,
Men with guns on the horizon far behind you,
The past tense threatening your presence.

I hear a concert of AK47s click, as thousands
Reload. The heat is tremendous – you have a radio.
But the sound of sand lifting from the ground
In the grip of the wind, disturbs – you understand what is
      happening,
Not through sight but through the sounds.
I could almost hear you, your breathing
As you gave birth again and another sister
Opened her eyes. Her wet face of sand.

In the drawing of this drama, the mist of mystery
Rising above the airwaves and heatwaves
We have scattered around the world,
Revolutions between us. Implosions of conscience.
Corrupting earthquakes have split our family – between us
Swallows migrate above the Atlantic Ocean
Pixellating the sky on tidal waves of heat
With such damnable ease.

And amongst the purple rain and stormy airwaves
Radio waves like flocks of swallows or the flamingos of
       Lake Tana
That seem to fly out from the reflecting solar wind
Land upon both of us with feather-wing ease,
Bringing my world to yours and your world to mine.
And now that we meet,
The sand storm lays low.
       Like a pride of lions
       After the chase,
The sun rises, its golden mane shakes.
You tell me, 'I heard a poem on the World Service,'
And I finally, face to face, get to tell you
It was *me*

Tuning in through the hissing noise
To you tuning in to me.

RICOCHET

A man shot a man who was a father,
The son of the dead father shot the father of the other son
Who was the man who had shot the first father.
Then I was born – I was told it didn't matter
'Cause time had passed.

But my uncle who was holding the pain
Of his dead brother – who was my father –
Said he couldn't forgive because every year,
Every minute of every day he loved his brother
And consequently there was a score to settle.

I am living here because there was a revolution
And some say this was why the man killed the father in
The first place – our family lost our property.
But I can go back – I am a man now.

The son of the neighbour who was the original killer
Was living in our house at home, said that he owned it now.
My uncle travelled back, to our homeland, but no longer,
No longer felt at home in his own homeland. He took a gun
Which was owned by an old friend of the counter-revolution
And shot himself. And the neighbour who was the son of
The man who I was told was a killer told me, at his funeral
That his dad hadn't shot first that my dad had.

DOCUMENTARY

This is – face blurred to defend identity
And he says – actor's voice
These are his friends – faces blurred to protect identity
And his parents – actors' voices, faces blacked out
Who live near – not real name of town
Who drive – licence plate obscured
Have said that they believe their son – face blurred to
       defend identity
Will return to – not real village name
But they will keep looking for – not real name.
The father – actor's voice – says he is
Innocent of the social services charges – actor's voice.
The events in this report have been changed to protect the
       identity
Of those included.
If you have any information about – blurred face, fictitious
       name
And you live in – fictitious village to protect parents
Then please contact us at – blurred number.

EVERY DAY LIVING

Another day flies, another brother dies,
Another mother haunts her home with her own cries,
Another man falls to another chant and call
From another racist neighbour behind another thin wall.

Another sleeps well through another night of hell,
Another tranquilliser and no one can tell
That yet another dream was not what it seemed,
More a paper veil for a hollow of screams.

Another sister flies from the building in the skies
Clutching another catalogue of clothes she couldn't buy.
Another suicide, another broken inside,
Another written letter for the parents to hide.

Another dream shatters as another man batters
Hope from the eyes of a woman that matters.
Another crack alarm, another track in the arm,
Another vein hides from another shot of calm.

Every day living, every day I give in,
Every day I wake up to a new beginning.

EMAIL

I shall be totally honest with you
And mean all that I say, *Delete Undo*
Without you I am incomplete,
Less of the man I know I am. *Delete*
Less your heart, mine won't beat but burn
Delete Delete Delete Return.

ELEPHANT IN THE ROOM

It isn't what's said, it's what's not said
What says it all.
The day you brought it home
I'll never forget.
It was only seven foot tall then.
An elephant! I said.
Put it in the back yard.
Fine, you said, *Fine!*
And disgruntled
Tied it to the washing line.

As you slept I'd pull back the curtains
Stand by the window and watch it.
A dark shadow. An iceberg. A hump filled the back yard,
Rising and falling with each deep gentle snore.

Breakfasts were never the same again.
The elephant took up all the space
And had no table manners whatsoever,
Although it was useful for the washing-up.
Whenever I broached the subject
You'd rant and rave and fume,
Say I was going crazy, *There is no elephant in the room.*

But the saddest thing is not the crockery it smashed
Nor the walls it demolished, of our past.

It wasn't its footsteps stamped all over our home,
The cracked floorboards or its wont to roam.
It was the lie established after I said, *It's there.*
For years you looked at me and said, *Where, dear, where?*

ARCHITECTURE

Each cloud wants to be a storm
My tap water wants to be a river
Each match wants to be an explosive
Each reflection wants to be real
Each joker wants to be a comedian
Each breeze wants to be a hurricane
Each drizzled rain wants to be torrential
Each laugh from the throat wants to burst from the belly
Each yawn wants to hug the sky
Each kiss wants to penetrate
Each handshake wants to be a warm embrace.
Don't you see how close we are to crashes and confusion,
Tempests and terror, mayhem and madness,
and all things out of control?

Each melting ice cube wants to be a glacier
Each goodbye wants to be the smooth stroke of a forehead
Each cry wants to be a scream
Each carefully pressed suit wants to be creased
Each midnight frost wants to be a snow drift
Each mother wants to be a friend
Each night-time wants to strangle the day
Each wave wants to be tidal
Each subtext wants to be a title
Each winter wants to be the big freeze
Each summer wants to be a drought

Each polite disagreement wants to be a vicious denial
Each diplomatic smile wants to be a one-fingered tribute
        to tact.
Don't you see how close we are to crashes and confusion,
Tempests and terror, mayhem and madness,
and all things out of control?

        Keep telling yourself.
        You've got it covered.

THE LETTER

It was a perfectly poisonous letter
Delivered on a perfectly poisonous day,
The postman dressed in black top hat and tails
Slow marched the street.

Five midnight-black musicians played the horn section
And wept theatrically between notes. Neighbours threw
    petals
And the police cordoned off the area for the procession.
The po-faced postman, cheeks high, nose long, eyes small,
Had risen to the occasion with the reverence of a priest
Or mock respect of a drunk.

The gate which with gloved hand he opened never
    screamed before as then;
It was a cry more than a squeak. A scream more than a cry.
A howl more than a scream.
His solemn face raised an eyebrow and lowered an eye,
Neighbours' curtains crossed their hearts and hoped to die.
He held the brown envelope aloft as if it were the sentence.

My garden path was lined with weeping pretend relatives
With dancing handkerchiefs. A curling crowd of cloud
    walked across the sky.
From inside I watched the letterbox open and saw the
    postman's eyes

He slipped it through and I watched it glide like a knife
And stutter through the air and rest on the hall carpet,
A perfectly poisonous letter delivered
On a perfectly poisonous day.

MOLASSES AND LONG SHADOWS

How the long shadows stretch a life in a day
How the tall sweet reeds of sugar cane sway
How the sun set on the blazing empire
How the wind of change carried fire
And stench. The sweet sticky scent of molasses
In the scorched sky as its night-time passes.
The world slumps awake and opens its eyes.
Free women, rise up, free men, rise.

Out of the strong came something to eat
From the most powerful came something sweet
What stronger than a lion? What sweeter than honey?
What can't be bought but is the making of money
Riddled with riddles like chains riddles rattle
The middle passage and its cheated chattel.
My word is my bond, my bind. I am bound
To abolish myth and all it surrounds.

Plantation mist's rise – the strangest fruit reveals
Guilt-riddled Cain in the sugar cane fields,
But these are stakes wrenched through the wretched.
Oh, the sweeping serrated shadows stretched.
And of war less recent we say, lest we forget,
Here grows the unforgettable and yet
The families who sowed this rotting crop
Reap its benefits today and, no wonder, forgot.

How the long shadows stretch a life in a day
How the tall sweet reeds of sugar cane sway
How the sun sets on the blazing empire
How the wind of change carried the fire
And the black ashes blew dark as molasses
And though time runs through us spirit surpasses
As the world wakes and opens its eyes
Free men, rise up, free women, rise.

MOVING MOUNTAINS

I climbed a mountain for her
Then saw a frown upon her.
She said I only climbed up here
So I could look back down on her.

MANCHESTER PICCADILLY

These eyes are the windows to my soul,
Before them Piccadilly dreams unfold.
This city of freedom, of future, of fame.
I catch a dream, catch a pathway, a plane,
I got Piccadilly mapped upon my skin.
I got her reflection shining out from within.
I got my coffee to go in the place I stay.
I got what's coming tomorrow, today.

I got all that I need here in the palm of my hand.
Every time Piccadilly grows I expand
Reflected in these windows, the eyes to my soul,
The discovery, the cave of gold.
I got Piccadilly in my heart, in my veins,
I get high from her hope, from her name.
From the mirrored buildings that scrape the sky
I got the hard sell and the good buy.

I got it all here. I got it all at my fingertips.
I let the words flower from my tongue's tip,
I got this city mapped into my skin.
I take it all easy but I take it all in,
I got these pathways these patterns within.
I take it all easy. I take it all in.
I hear the sound of hope, its truest tone.
I got Piccadilly. I got the city. I got home.

I got this A to Z in my head. It's like I said,
Here are my waking dreams, my bed.
I got these reflections of outside, within,
I take it all easy I take it all in.
I got these designs inside my mind,
I got the power of reason, of the line,
I got all that I need here in the palm of my hand.
Every time Piccadilly grows, I expand.

REMEMBERING THE GOOD TIMES WE NEVER HAD

These are the days of long nights
Where the washing-up piles up
And the tide mark on the bath
Laughs at the man in the mirror.
The lock's broke and the sink chokes
On soggy bread; it's dead round here.

Beer sucks the carpet
From last night's cans and programmes
Not unlike the night before,
Nor the night before the night before.
Sitcoms – seen one, seen 'em all,
Seven thirty roll call at the East End.
And the Street, there's no end.
I nearly died when Deirdre cried.
I nearly cried when Deirdre died.

The phone rang and I sang
To the tune of a man pretending. It's never-ending,
I put the blues in with the whites,
Set the frying pan alight,
Burnt the toast, began to roast the oven.
Left the water running over the sink
As I began to think
Of the man who grew terminally mad
Thinking of the good times that we never had.

I'm all loose ends and U-bends,
All back-to-back and cul-de-sac.
Gone the wrong way up a one-way street,
With too much weight on my sleeve.
There is no room in my room
Except that is for the vacuum
Where the laughter that we sorely missed
And sparkling conversation that never happened,
Where the wild slippy sex that seemed to just grate
And coming home drunk and laughing and late,
Swilled in my delirious head.
When I was with you, didn't we play dead?

I'm caught in the warp, I need to sort
The blue jeans from the white shorts.
I'm all T-shirts and T-junctions, can't function,
And the only light from the end of this tunnel
Is from my torch. I look back and it's just as bad,
Enough to drive a sane man mad,
Remembering the good times that we never had.

SOME THINGS I LIKE

(A poem to shout)

I like wrecks, I like ex-junkies,
I like flunks and ex-flunkies,
I like the way the career-less career,
I like flat beer,
I like people who tell half stories and forget the rest,
I like people who make doodles in important written tests,
I like being late. I like fate. I like the way teeth grate,
I like laceless shoes cordless blues,
I like the one-bar blues,
I like buttonless coats and leaky boats,
I like rubbish tips and bitten lips,
I like yesterday's toast,
I like cold tea, I like reality,
I like ashtrays, I write and like crap plays.

I like curtains that don't quite shut,
I like bread knives that don't quite cut,
I like rips in blue jeans,
I like people who can't say what they mean,
I like spiders with no legs, pencils with no lead,
Ants with no heads, worms that are half dead.
I like holes, I like coffee cold. I like creases in neat folds.
I like signs that just don't know where they're going,
I like angry poems,
I like the way you can't pin down the sea.
See.

THE MAN IN THE HOSPITAL

At the hospital there is a man who walks the corridors
In nightclothes through the deadly night's shade.
I have watched him from my bed the past five months
Pretending to be asleep. Sleep is where I pretend
Morning will come.

I have come to know the sand paper sound
Of silence scarred by his dragging, drugged feet.
I have come to know the sound of his mumbling
Stumbling words spoken as he steps
Through strips of moonlight, broken.
He walks through the shadow of the valley of breath.
Surrounded by the incoming outgoing air of the dying,
Of *us* waiting to exhale and bated to inhale.

I am tired. So tired. So. Tired.
My bed is covered with fresh grass and night sweats:
Dew, my dog, a Red Setter, deft and gentle, steps through
          the ward.
She pitter-patters her way past the other beds,
Hunches her shoulders and dives upwards onto mine.
She stretches by my feet – a nightingale stings.
I am surrounded by breathing, it is the sound of the sea.
He is coming. He is coming; I hear his shuffling feet.
I raise my eyelid slightly;

It takes tremendous effort. The effort of the Egyptians
Pulling the stones to the pyramid at sunrise. I raise my eyes.

He's at the door of the ward facing forward.
He stares straight ahead. A head. Straight. Stares.
There is no illness. There is no illness.
No AIDS! There is no such illness.
The others wake too, too tired to argue,
To hear the tears in his lies, the lies in his tears;
To see the fear in his eyes through the eye of his fears.

*** * * *** THIS

* * * * this, *** * * *** all that
Who the *** * * *** are you shouting at?
* * * * you and what you're shouting for
* * * * you all, I don't care no more
* * * * it, you are the dead loss
* * * * you and *** * * *** your *** * * *** ing boss
Not much to say, no *** * * *** er to tell
* * * * * * * * * * * * it *** * * *** in' hell

THE LOST KEY

I know, if you knew when you lost it you wouldn't be looking.
Have you checked the back of the sofa? Underneath it?
Could it be in your pockets? Have you checked your pockets?
What about your pockets? What about there, in there?
No. The insides of your pockets. Now, have you got,
Have you got any inside pockets? The insides of the inside.
I mean your inside pocket. Inside your inside pocket.

Have you checked the cupboards? With the clothes in,
The clothes, the new clothes, 'cause you never know,
Things turn up in the strangest . . . They do. Turn up.
You have to check all of the pockets in all of the clothes
Of all the places you've ever been – that's a lot of pockets.

Find out where the new land lies and the old lies land.
Funny how when you're looking you find everything else
Except. Don't start blaming people. Before you know it
You'll accuse everyone that is nearest to you,
Everyone that was closest to you, that mattered.
You'll turn on them, investigate them for the time
They might have slipped it in their pockets
And slipped away saying goodbye, goodbye.
Have you checked your pockets? Your inside pockets?

MAGPIE

I saw a single magpie,
It really got to my head.
I thought, 'You unlucky bastard,'
And shot the bugger dead.

BEFORE WE GET INTO THIS

Before we get to know each other
And sing for tomorrow
And unearth yesterday
So that we can prepare our joint grave
You should know that I have no family,
Neither disowned nor distanced – none.

No birthdays nor Christmas,
No telephone calls. It's been that way
Since birth for what it's worth
No next of skin.

I am the guilty secret of an innocent woman
And a dead man – tell your parents, they'll want to know.

DORIS

I see the cattle float by and the window break,
I see the dog spin on the coach and the clock wait,
And I think to myself what a wonderful world.

I see skies of red and eyes in fright,
The clammy day, the dark scared night,
And I think to myself what a wonderful world.

The colours of my daughter so pretty in the sky,
I see her in the faces in every girl passing by,
I see friends shaking, shouting 'What can we do?'
I see my daughter again mouthing, 'I love you.'

I hear my new baby crying, I'll watch her grow.
She'll never see her sister passed but she'll know.
And I'll think to myself what a wonderful world.

FLAGS

These pavement cracks are the places
Where poets pack their warrior words,
Where insects have the Olympic races,
Where seeds slip from embittered birds,
Where vert valleys cling to ledges,
Where sliding silver rivers run.
These pavement cracks are the places
Where violent valleys swallow sun.

These pavement cracks are the places
Where shadows of moving bridges flow,
Where rain rushes rock faces,
Where heat crouches from the cold,
Where dying dust of dreams slide,
Where silt turns into food,
Where home truths confide,
And secret silent worries brood.

And perhaps these pavement cracks
Are the patterns of concrete butterflies
Where thoughts carefully cultivated
Wait to wake, grow wings and fly.
Perhaps these pavement cracks
Hold pieces of the Manchester myriad,
The people of a modern earth.
This world between the windswept flags.

INTIMATE ANGER

Before the silenced vase hits the floor
Before the slam of the door in the corridor
Before the crying curtains draw
Before the slow and singular applause
Between the lines of the clause

Before the knife splits the skin
Before the pick of the skin
Before the accusation of sin
Before the cheat claims the win

I am immersed in anger
Intimate as the cold lake
That grows on my chest.

ADVICE FOR THE LIVING

Dead fast this.
Everyone's dying to arrive,
Living for deadlines, trying to
Stay straight as a die. They'll get
There, dead or alive because they're
Dead set, and they do arrive in shores
Of dead heats, dead beats at dead ends
Dead messed up like dead stock. The living
Dead flogging dead horses in the dead of
Night. Dead right dead lost dead right.
Every now and again we stop dead
In our tracks, dead still 'cause it's
Dead hard, like a dead weight's
Dropped on the head ... wouldn't
You die for a little piece, die for
A breath of hope? Dead right,
I would. In the dead centre of
All this deadlocking, dread
Locked. Words, dead ahead.
They read: *Life is not worth*
living if there's no one that you
would die for. Dead right.

IN THE KINGDOM OF THE BLIND

In the Kingdom of the Blind the one-eyed man is a fool
And useless; incredibly pathetically and fantastically useless.
He wastes all precious time trying to convince us
How wonderful sight is and how much we may *use* him
In this light he names every object in minutiae.
Everything has a description, he tells us, *everything quantifiable*.
He has the gall to work out somehow that he is a king because
In the Kingdom of the Blind apparently the one-eyed man
        is king.

In the Kingdom of the Blind the one-eyed man is a fool,
A babbling pompous self-obsessed fool.
We stopped listening to the poor man a long long time ago.
But how could he hear us not listening.
He certainly could not *see* us not listening.
We noticed over the years his voice developed a quiver
It was as if he was spitting words out
Against his will. Then he disappeared . . .

I hear he became rabid while shouting a fantastic articulation
Of the froth that curled from his mouth and scabs that clung
        to his knuckles.
Thoughts stampeded like wolfpacks through his head, he said.
I hear he tried to run away from his own descriptions into
        the forests and fields;

Describing every twig, every grass whiplash, every cloud form
Until he reached 'the cool and silent hills'. He described them
        without pause.

We could smell him from far on the other side of the kingdom.
I hear he found a seat beneath a hanging baobab tree
Where no one could see him. He described how alone he was
'cept for the creeping baobab shadow, the crickets and sepia
        sunlight.
My single unblinking eye stares forward at the gold sunlight
Bouncing from the sheer metal point of the dagger which hovers
Gripped by my steady hand, before my eyelashes.

In the Kingdom of the Blind the one-eyed man is a fool.

INSPIRATION

Imagination has a fingerprint,
Each dream is a new template,
Each emotion has contours;
Add inspiration and create.

You say this is too far away,
This is not in your command.
It is! It's as close to you
As the fingers on your hand.

OLYMPIC INVOCATION

TUNE IN

Not a poetry picnic for the bards to enthrall
But Poetry Olympics at The Festival Hall.
The only metres run will be the meter of line,
The only high jump they'll get is if they run over time.

AND SWITCH OVER

And a man like a bomb flies down the wing
– flies down the wing.
On a wing and a prayer
Tiptoes through the lion's lair,
Cuts through the defence, dessicates the attack
And scores a goal – 'Poetry, poetry,' Jimmy Hill growls.

SWITCH BACK

And a weatherman – a closet poet if ever there was one –
Performs his piece, words swill as arm sweeps:
'A sleeping rain and a quiet mist,
A touch of thunder will brood in the night
And the blackened ice will melt by morning light.'

SWITCH OVER

And an advert broadcasts a poet in a wheelchair,
John Betjeman catches the wind in his hair.
Asked if he had any regrets,
'Yes,' he said, 'not enough sex.'

Rhyming couplets ring to entice – it's
Poetry in adverts and we don't realise
It's in birthday cards, in the papers each week,
It's poetry we think and imperfectly speak –

It's poetry on gravestones, in nursery rhymes,
Poetry in documentaries that document times.
It's poetry on buses and poems on tubes
And in the printed matter whether it matters or not
            to you.
It's poems in the prayer books and on the protest
            marches,
Poetry sprayed in aerosol underneath the arches.

Chill out – tune in, as they might have said.
Poetry is life – without it you're dead.

SALT MIND

When the waters dip and return to the sea
Like an army of embittered white wolves,
She counts the crystals they left over.
These are how many tears dropped.
She lives in this salt mind,
She sculpts a life-sized family
From those salt crystals.
We sit together for days;
I watch her as the wind spits sand at me.

As the tide retracts her wounds open.
She clutches her sculpture and screams.
She tries to turn tides from her salt mind
But the confident sea is walking back up the beach
To repatriate its children,
To welcome them into its soaking arms,
To drag them by its teeth into the Atlantic.

She's taken to eating the sculpture
Rather than let them go.
She spews into the tide
Jerking like a beached dolphin.
I have watched from the grass dunes for too long,
Been waved away too many times,
The weather's worn into my face,

Revealing the wet black sea rocks beneath.
I turn my back on the tide
And hear her splashing water.

SIGNS

Emergency Exit. Mind your Head.
Managing Director. Changing Rooms.
Rocks Falling. Rocks Falling.
Level Crossing. Zebra Crossing.
Pelican Crossing. Stop Children Stop.
One Way. One Way. Dual Carriageway.
No Exit. Wide Load. Subsidence.
Slow Speed. Slow Speed. No Exit.
Maximum Headroom. Road Works Ahead.
Rocks Falling. Rocks Falling.

THE SHADOW OF THE LABURNUM

You said that I shouldn't eat the laburnum seeds,
Though they tasted good they were poisonous.
These words ran through me like excited children
And finally panting they arrived back in their place
In the following wide-eyed and expectant order –
Poisonous laburnum seeds, they tasted good though.

Cross-legged in the garden I had my fill of worms
Surrounded by yellow flowers and seeds
That carpeted the sharp glass green grass.
One by one I started to pick the seeds out
Until they became a huddle of a puddle in my palm
And carefully I popped a good twenty in,
Crunchy – nice. I swallowed with great drama
Then without thought it was back to the worms.

The laburnum lay its evening shawl on the garden
Thousands of iron filings twisted in my stomach
My throat-hole shrunk, I couldn't swallow, nor scream,
I dry-retched and my back stiffened,
I dragged and splashed through the yellow sea
Of laburnum flowers leaving a dark green wake.
I was splashing and flowers were sticking to my sweat,
I was drowning beneath the summer shadow of the laburnum

And I hadn't heard the barrel twist as the oiled bolt choked the
Mouth of the front-door frame nor you holding your breath
On the other side.

THE BATTLE OF ADWA, 1896

Preceding Adwa

Remember this, the Europeans
Carved up our homes with blood thirst,
Not because we were the Third World
But because we were the First.
Because we held gold in our hearts,
Because we had diamonds for eyes,
Because oil ran through our veins,
And a blessing hung in our skies.

Remember, that when they scrambled
In the conference in Berlin
And callously carved Africa
Searing each African's skin
It was not just because of their greed
Or need to sow seeds saturated with sorrow,
But because through Africa's greatness
They envisioned their own great tomorrow

The Beginning

Baratieri, the Italian general, had ice instead of eyes
And a tongue of five leather whips
Ras Alula was deafened by the whisper

Of lies that seeped from his lips.
Through Alula's agents who could read
The tone of Ethiopian winds,
Their whisper *We will catch the Italian advance*
Before the advance begins.
And with anger, that of lions,
And a swiftness of eagles' wings,
Alula rose magnificent and rode
To the foot of Menelik the king;
With all their five generals, Menelik growled,
Five armies and damned attacks,
It will take one strong Ethiopia
To break their stiffened backs.

Meantime with pomp and primitive greed
The Italians embarked on their plan;
They left for Adwa from Entisco
With night-time a shroud for each man.
Unbeknown every step was recorded
By Alula's silent speedy spies
Who traced the battalion's movement
Through the reflections they left in the sky.
The Italians noting the Ethiopian dawn
As a cloak for the surprise attack
Had no knowledge that warriors were waiting
And would give the surprise back.
With all their five generals, Ras Alula whispered,

Their armies and planned attacks,
It will take one strong Ethiopia
To break their brittle backs.

The War

The Ethiopians advanced from below,
A hero's sacrifice for a country's love
Suffice as they fell and blood spilled
For another flank to reign from above,
And so unveiled complex manoeuvres
Of hope and honour for history
Whose aim the breaking of evil
And the waking of victory.
The Ethiopians from all provinces
Gathered with truth as protection
Descended around Adwa with justice and honour
And unity as their weapon.
The cracking snapping of rattling rifles
Awoke the morning sun;
From ridges the Italians poured fire
The Battle of Adwa begun:

With all their five generals Ras Mengesha fought,
With their armies and their attacks.

It will take one strong Ethiopia
To snap their stiffened backs.

The Victory

It seemed the more Ethiopians were killed
Then twice as many returned.
The more they tried to drench their spirits
The more the spirits burned.
It seemed as if amongst the red mist
Each man that fell wounded rose again,
Each breath of air rejuvenated his lungs,
Each drop of blood seeped back to his veins.
It seemed that the Ethiopians
Rose from the river beds,
Came from the shadows of mountainsides,
With eyes of stone and dread,
And Baratieri's generals sensing
The beginning of the end
Succumbed to the deafening whisper,
Surrender, surrender.

Remember this: It was not one of Ethiopia
But Ethiopia as one;
It was not part of the sum that won
But part of everyone.
It was not the heart on its own
But its veins that pumped on.

It was not just the warriors
But where they were all from.
Remember this: how the story washed
Across the continent enslaved
Flooded with the story of Adwa
In a whispered tidal wave
From Kenya to Senegal
From Morocco to the Gambia.
The liberation began in Adwa, 1896,
And ended in South Africa.

THE GILT OF CAIN

Here is the *ask price* on the *closed position*,
History is no inherent acquisition
For here the *technical correction* upon the act,
A *merger* of truth and in *actuals* fact,
On the *spot*, on the money – the *spread*.
The *dealer* lied when the *dealer* said,
The *bull* was charging, the *bear* was dead,
The market must calculate *per capita*, not head.

And great traders *acting in concert*, arms rise
As the *actuals* fraught on the sea of *franchise*
Thrown overboard into the *exchange* to drown
In distressed *brokers'* disconsolate frown.
In *accounting liquidity* is a mounting morbidity
But raising the arms with such rigid rapidity . . .
Oh, the reaping, the raping rapacious *fluidity*,
The violence, the vicious and vexed *volatility*.

The roaring trade floor rises above crashing waves:
The traders buy ships, beneath the slaves.
Sway machete back, sway machete again,
Crick crack *cut back* the Sugar Rush, Cain.
The *whipsaw*, it's all and the whip saw it all,
The *rising market* and the cargo fall.
Who'll enter 'Jerusalem', make the *margin call* for Abel.
Who will kick over the stall and turn the table.

Cain gathers cane as *gilt*-gift to his land,
But whose sword of truth shall not sleep in hand?
Who shall unlock the *stocks and share*,
Break the *bond*, the bind unbound – lay bare
The truth? *Cash flow* runs deep but spirit deeper,
You ask the question, 'Am I my brother's keeper?'
I answer the best way *I* can, through laws.
My name, my brother, Wilberforce.

APPLECART ART

Upset the art, smash the applecart,
Sell it for firewood to warm hearts.
Don't join the loop, the loop troupe,
Don't hump through their hoops
Or get stuck on sticky peaks of double speak.
I'm clocking the click of the clique.
I swim with the shallow.
If they demand I be deep
Though, I can hold my breath
Deeper than sleep, deeper than death.

Upset the art, crash the snapplecart,
Sell it for cash and a brand new start.
Turn cart wheels on the art wheels
If that's how your heart feels.
To those who demand you stand by their pandect,
Call them all cheats on call and collect,
They're gargoyles hunched on their haunches,
Stalking the walk at lunches and launches.
They backbite, backslap, salubriously clap
With cleaver hands to stick in the back.

Upset the art, trash the cattlecart,
Start the stampede in the heart of the art.
Don't play poker with the mediocre,

Token-filled pack full of jokers.
The Class A offenders are pretenders
Protecting their pretence, return them to sender.

Feel fierce flocks of fight forming and flowing,
Know you're only as good as your last poem.
Cut yourself, it should be ink you're bleeding,
Know you're only as good as your last reading.
Let wisdom be the weight of your wealth
And your greatest competitor, yourself.

I WILL NOT SPEAK ILL OF THE DEAD

In the orchard I catch a falling leaf and wish to make no wish.
Before my eyes the leaf, a veined slither of heart, pulsates.
A collar-boned branch snaps beneath or behind or within
But I am here for a reason and cannot wait to leave.

I won't speak ill of the dead.
Not a word as I reach, twist, then with a tug of the wrist
Pick the scarlet fruit from the bitter memory tree.
The sound of a hiss pours down in a shiver and circles me.
This is not fruit for eating. This bulbous leathery bruised
Over-sized bull's eye, a cross between a lychee and an apple,
Seeps sticky brown oil that coils into my half-formed fist.

I am told this flesh is poisonous and so it is my service
That I should bring it to my mouth beneath my nose,
Smell and draw the decaying cancerous tinge.
Slow but deliberate I sink my teeth into its stringy slime
And feel the cold flesh slide up my teeth and onto my gums.
The first bite is the worst bite and the brown oil slides
Down my chin as the mulch slips within me.

This is good. I am impervious to the poison because
I was fed the seeds of this tree when I slept as a child.
It grows inside me. I feel its branches stretch inside
And at night-time sometimes I hear it tear my inner flesh.

Though a hand has become one deformed knot
The other holds a wooden pen.

I won't *speak* ill of the dead. Not a word.
There will be nothing more satisfying than knowing that
The sewage with all its pips and dangerous seeds
Will be dragged away from me, spat out into the sea
A long way away – I will not speak ill of the dead.
Not a word.

TRANSISTOR

Airwaves transmit, vocals translate,
Emotions in transit transmigrate,
Story transmutes and what transpires
Are transfinite transonic choirs.
The soldier, the teacher, the lover, the storm,
Translocate, transform.

THIS TRAIN (SING ALONG)

This train is bound for Wigan, this train
This train is bound for Wigan, this train
This train is bound for Wigan
Praise the lord 'cause it's a big 'un
This train is bound for Wigan, this train.

MOLTEN

Don't let them tell you any different,
That you are not made from molten rock,
That you were not born in waves
Amongst the morning mist
Until you solidified and became.

Blindfolded they pat your face.
They frown confused and see darkness,
And tell you with a wagging finger
That you may be a dealer of death
Or a thief in their night.

They're too blind to see the sky-wonder in your eyes
And those pupils, those small spinning worlds,
Which they are caught in. Remember,
They revolve like specks of dust
Around such an incredible world –
They may sting your cataracts –
But don't let the tears that *will* fall
Drown the reason they fell.
For then you will truly have drowned.

HORIZONS

Sparks. Sparks spiral from the foundry –
The future is being forged, tomorrow built for today.
Stars. Each morning we hoist the sun on golden ropes
Into the sky, in all its molten glory
                    Welcome to the world!

The builder of the rainbow understands the rain;
The raiser of the sun knows the weight of light;
The listener of horizons knows the sound of vision.
In these finite measurements – the crux of the creative –
From this complex calculus arise the line drawings of vision;
                    The architecture of aspiration,
                    The mathematics of motivation.

Pulling the sun into the sky through the hard day's night,
Shedding light so shadows bow in grace: the people –
The heart of all architecture, pumping the economy through
                    The great arteries of the region.

Hoist. Hoist. Hoist. Hoist.
As liquid light pours across the contours
Each morning what were dreams themselves,
What were pastures of premonition,
What were the sketches of vision
                    Become reality absolute
                    And bear fruit.

DEI MIRACOLE

   The spirit of structure can't be foreseen,
For somewhere between
  The architecture and the dream
    More than the sum of its parts
Somehow, somewhere, the heart.

CHRISTMAS

Christmas can be split into two kinds of people –
Those who look into the windows of houses of others
And those who look out.

CATCHING NUMBERS

Since the first journey on public transport
All aboard the womb. First stop, The Doctor's Arms
To this wonderful wet morning in July,
The thought of the number thirty-two was
The most fantastic thought of all the thoughts
That all the thoughts could think, I thought.
Not even the most important age of sixteen
Was as monumental as the number thirty-two.

A rainbow sprayed itself across the city,
It was three minutes to two. Three whole minutes to two –
Step by step and stop by stop, *tick tock tick tock*.
Turning the corner in all its double-decked glory
The galleon thundered down the main road,
Its captain at the wheel stern and concentrated.

The closer it got the smaller I became.
With a ripple of fear I held out my hand
And it growled to a gigantic concrete churning
Kerb-rippling road-gripping High Street halt.
Tick tock the double-decker docked.

Never had I felt more powerful than then.
At sixteen years old stopping a number thirty-two,
A traveller to my dreams and a passenger to my fate,
Not a second too early nor a minute too late.

RED SKY DAWN

Do the children inside pregnant women sleep?
And if they do, then do they dream?
And if they do, then what?
This was not a night for dreams.
And tide and time wait for no woman.
She'll know the storm. It is the birth
And if this is so then pregnancy is the calm before.
And it's the most terrifying thing, this calm.

She senses the rising tide *from* inside
And hears the shhhhhhhhhh of oncoming rain.
She smells the sodden earth carried in air.
Her breathing has changed. It is the wind.
Her breath has become the wind.
And her skin has changed. It is the earth.
And she swears that if she put her hand on the ground
Moss might grow on her wrists, crows would nest in her hair
And if she screams the world would shake and men cry.

The storm is here. The storm is here
Smashing the windowsills and locking the doors.
She passes children through broken glass
Into the sky, into tomorrow and she's filling with water
– can barely breathe as the room swims around her.
She sees father and mother and her grandmother all
The wall clock spins away on selfish waves.

She prays her children will hold on till tomorrow comes . . .
But her daughter, swims through that window and never
returns.

And as she saw this passing, she knew what it was to be a
woman:
To lose something and gain something in the same word,
To be the centre of all things and on the perimeter,
To be all-powerful and all-vulnerable.
And in that moment the mourning, the red sky dawn
Through the wreath, good grief, another . . . A child's born.

WINTER: SHEPHERD'S WARNING

The clothes on the wash-line, limp and still,
A renegade spit of rain races through enemy lines
And crashes on a dustbin lid. Telltale signs.
Echoes ricochet around the estate in opposite directions,
Alsatians run in circles chasing their tails.
Confused birds fall with wings of sycamore seeds.
She creeps carefully with menace wrapped in cloak of silence,
Twisting in the scowling face, the breathless body,
The weakening pulse of the sky.
Hold onto your children or they'll be swept away
Down the dark rivers of your High Street
Or dragged by the wind up the sides of skyscrapers –
Red sky of a morning shepherd's warning.

This wind wades through the waves of the sky
And marches onto blood-splattered beaches towards us.
Her bitter breath in the strains of air. Cold chills spill.
Sound the alarm. Hold onto your loved ones.
Call your friends, tell them, *Don't come around. Stay in.*
There are disappearances in Dogger.
Raging seas in Rockall.

She will slip into houses, crawl the stairs of the frail,
Grip necks as we sleep. She will suffocate them.
I hear the choking sound of the hidden. The rain applauds.

Grown trees cackle, snap and whip as wooden coffins
Squeeze through nervous doors,
Spades plunge into the crisp flesh of earth.
Red sky of a morning – shepherd's warning.

The veins of the sky have burst.
Weather reporters are in flak jackets.
Cliffs with their chests plucked out cry wet stone tears
Into the panicking and frantic sea.
Trees with their hair pulled towards the sky have
Innards torn out and cut from the ground. Take your children.
The storm is here. The storm is here. The storm is here.

Thunder preaches from the pulpit, faces leak
From the brilliant cracks in the sky, lunging
Spiked arms. The end is nigh! The end is nigh!
All the christs and all the gods have been released,
All the devils and all the demons and
All the plagues and all the diseases, and all the spirits
And all the ghosts. Released. Released. Released.

Keep your windows closed. Wrap up warm
And fall into dreams in this mantra, hugging plastic bottles
Of boiling water, through dreams of swimming in tears.
And the tears become the dark leaves of autumn
And the dark leaves become wet tongues and the wet tongues
A storm-filled sea. In the morning when my neck bursts

Through the surface and I grasp for breath, a bright warm light
Punches through my darkness, there is nothing but a reddened
      battlefield
Of a sky and the muffled sounds of flocks of shepherds.
Red sky in the morning – shepherd's warning.

SPRING: MAYDAY MAYDAY

I can always tell when it's spring. There's this plane crash
And it happens to crash into our house.
It's as sure a sign as any sign is.
I step into the kitchen and there it is: the wreckage.
Thick girders of light split the house from every direction.
Half the plane's fuselage is in the sink, soaked in hot oil,
Tick tick ticking – the sound of sulking metal cooling.
There's glass everywhere.

The pilot seat has stuck in the boiler. Again.
And a fountain of steam sprays bouquets of hissing greys.
A map in the corner tries to hide from the horror,
Its wet roads have spilled into rivers that have spilled into towns
That have fallen down the sides of valleys.
Postcards like doves flit through thick dusted light.
There's burst suitcases everywhere. Everywhere.
A sign stuck in the larder door reads 'Emergency Exit'.

I look up at the ceiling, the rotator blades have crashed through,
Drunkenly swirling oily smoke coils through the blue.
A tannoy sprawled on the washing machine, its neck snapped,
Wails to the floor where the cracked control panel is,
Where a mangle of oxygen feeder wires hiss their last breath.
The wing tips in the front room in the television screen,
Its red flashing light bleeding, the room ticks selfishly

And the curtains are blowing outside on a fractured
        windowsill.
The landing gear's in the garden, in the laburnum tree,
Its wheels still spinning. Doesn't even know it's landed.

Secrets and lies all over the place. Half-written postcards.
The emergency crews won't come. They say there's
'Too much radiation. There's too much friction.'
'It's all too dangerous,' they say. 'And anyway
A little spring cleaning'll sort it all out.'

So here I am
As the laburnum tree twists its yellow fingers
Around broken pieces of plane; it's that time of year again.
I can smell it in the rain. It's the time of year to clean it all up;
It's the time of year for the crash and the time of year to tidy
        it up;
To find new places to put the wreckage, to make ornaments
        maybe,
To find new places for burst luggage, to sew it up maybe,
Give it away, maybe. It's time to dig holes in the garden.
        To bury it!
Time of year to cover it all and grow new plants.
Until next year when the strange fruit bursts from the earth
Triumphant as afterlife and falls from the skies, as if *real*.
That's how I know it's spring. See. See.
I woke this morning to find the garden and my home a wreck.

Pieces of plane. Gnarled metal, glinting with dew
And sunrise painting the whole scene a metallic red.
It's spring again.

SUMMER: MOUNTAIN TOP

When I swam through oil-filled waters spat upon this
      bitter earth
When I saw a mother's crying face at that dying birth
When I walked through icy winds, when I slept on beds of snow
When I felt the leadened hail stone, swam against the ice flow

When thoughts were crucifixes, when nightmares grew
      from the ground
When screams were entwined in my every word, every sound
When wounds opened and bled salted tears
When every day passed away like it was a year

When lost in leech-filled forests, when I stood alone in storms
When battered and tired from the day I was born
When the darkness enveloped me as the sun had gone away,
I carried on for the reason that I would reach here one day.

I would see spirits playing twister and by the sky streams
I would see layers of my own tears drift past like flocks of dreams
I would see glistening hope in every single teardrop of pain
And I would hear the sound of music in all this falling rain.

AUTUMN: LOST BRONZE

She waits in the forest and watches summer pass.
The rays dive through the canopy on golden ropes
And swim away through the air like shoals of golden fish.
Her smile is a farewell, a dignified goodbye
To the fading golden shoals of summer.

Sure as the sun rises and sure as the sun falls,
Sure as the rotted wood that turns to dust,
Sure as ashes to ashes and trust to trust,
The first cold breeze spills over her many shoulders
With all the forced tenderness of ownership.
The first breeze slips around her neck.
Kisses her bark bones and kisses the arches
That swoop beneath her arms.

Her capturer will waltz his princess before she sleeps.
She sways, limp at the mercy of the unwanted lover,
Devouring her body with invisible kisses of wind
Wrapping his breathy arms around her freezing torso.
The leaves that once sounded like beating wings
Cackle and crackle. They hiss like the fire in her
Stretching heart. The colours of burning are everywhere;
The oranges, the crimsons, the blood reds.
Sure as the rotted wood that turns to dust.
As ashes to ashes, trust to trust.

As packs of hungry grey lions the mist swills around her
　　　still feet.
Her castle is crumbling, the walls brought to their knees.
There are no tears as she throws down her jewels,
As chains break and slip from her neck,
Rings pulled nervously from her fingers,
Bracelets slipped from her slender wrists over veined hands,
Unclipped from her tensed ankles.

BARLEY FIELD

The barley field wished but swayed,
Washed by rain, dried by the sun
And combed by the wind.

The Oak stands, centre page,
I feel her stretch as morning pushes back the sheets.
Her leaves twist in the breeze like the hands
Of Indian dancers and the sun shoots through them,
Making shoals of golden fish swim through her shadow.

I was looking for inspiration and there it was.
Not in the field nor the sun nor the Oak,
Barely visible NG+DA – in the trunk.
I had been here before. The memory flooded back – surged.
And there I was in that sea of barley
Barely seeing you.

THE BOXER

For Phil Martin 1955–94

He saw riots scream and the blue sky scream
In the memory in smoke that lingered.
He saw furrowed frowns and nervous breakdowns
And outsiders who pointed their fingers.
They painted it blue and believed the news
That barks about the violence and crime.
He saw them scuttle like roaches, past him in coaches,
Their Moss Side is in their mind.

A boxer by trade and never afraid
Of the fingers that point at his home,
He built from foundations, made a soul nation
A palace grew from the stones.
He made princes kings, lords of the ring,
Made them swing like ballerinas on glass.
He taught inner strength and discipline
Peace and the power to last.

Governments came having heard the name
Of the man who built champions and dreams
Who against all the odds with his will and God's
Got to the top with the crop and the cream.
He made rights from wrong, made the weak strong,

Gave hope where it seemed there was none.
His legacy stands and lives on in this land
The Champ, the man, has gone.

TIME BOMB

When they took away his mother
He was determined to survive.
When he found his father dead
He clenched his breath to stay alive.

When they took away his name
He called himself free.
People close by would say
What a strong boy he must be.

When they took away his home
He found it in his heart.
And it only took a few more years
For it to blow his mind apart.

TORCH

One day you may find
That all is not dictated by time;
That a river is rushing through your head
Or a stampede of black doves from your eyes.

One day you may find that the ground
Which you once crawled on, learned to walk on, is sinking,
And the air that you drink in is hot
And there are no cul-de-sacs, just motorways with no signs,
Horizons with no hills or trees.

One day you may find that your small world
Is no longer so small
But a space too big to take in.
Out of your mind friends say *Hello*,
You are two minutes behind
And by the time they think you're a little weird, it's too late.
The letters you receive in the post
Are from the ghost of yourself
And you reflect on the defects and in effect
You are rejecting all that you ever were.

One day you may look in the mirror
And see into yourself,
All the tubes, holes and rushing hormones

Fighting each other for air with swords,
And one day you may bring yourself to yourself
And fight yourself until your soul lies
Like dead roses.

One day you may kick the shit out of yourself
To get out of the shit you've become.
One day you may face your mirror, falter in shock,
At what's looking back at you,
'cause that's not you!

One day you may fall on the floor
'cause the shit you are in has grown claws
And is gripping your neck.
You're a shipwrecked defect
Looking for a place to hide.

BBC

"The Queen's Speech"

BY LEMN SISSAY

Cast

The Queen	ADJOA ANDOH
Rabbi Hattenstone	DAVID HOROVITCH
Emtiaz Malik	ANJALI JAY
Cheryl Henderson	CARLA HENRY

Director – EOIN O'CALLAGHAN

NB: PLEASE BRING HARD-SOLED SHOES TO THE STUDIO

Recording:

Fri 17th November 2006, 0930 - 1230

THE SOUNDHOUSE STUDIOS
UNIT 11
GOLDHAWK INDUSTRIAL ESTATE
VINERY WAY
2a BRACKENBURY ROAD
LONDON
W6 0BA

Studio Managers:
Wilfredo Acosta - Panel

Editing:
Wilfredo Acosta
Soundhouse
Friday 17th November, 1330-1730

Broadcast Assistant:
James Robinson

Programme Number:

06DA3409LH0/1

Tape Number:

PLN646/06DA3409

TX Date:

Saturday 18th November 2006, 1900
and Sunday 19th November 2006, 1740

89

THE QUEEN SPEAKS:

I was born as you were born;
Curled into cloth as you were curled into cloth,
Washed with expectations as you were washed in expectations,
Born into a nation as you were born into a nation,
Born with a past as a present as you were born with a past,
Born to a mask as you were born into a mask,
Held as you were held and separated as you were.
I am one as you are one, as we are one, as one is born.

Our family is bound as your family is bound, by event;
Crowned by event. Are you not similar?
Carrying out the treaties and laws that went before? You,
Trudging back and forward carrying children from the well,
Passing on what you never knew you'd have to? Kith. Kin.
Are you not both victim and liberator of *your* origin,
The reluctant promoter of your blood line?

Carried out the treaties and laws that went before.
Have you not seen peace break out in your family *and* war?
Have you not cried at the blood shed in your name?
Have you not stood in the name of your blood with blame
On your hands? Have you not known in your family, shame
In the name of something bigger than you? And there,
Didn't people say how stoic you were?
They didn't see before you slept

The weeping. The pillow, wet.
My father, my mother like yours, waited.
They said I was what fate did.
For I was born as you were born – naked.

CHERYL HENDERSON:

Ma'am? They say I must call you ma'am, ma'am.
And I should bow. I am afraid to bow.
The identity card is written into my face.
I disappear each day I wake, without trace.
Your silence speaks an ocean. I am a boy in a boat
With no oars to row, speaking to you who rule the waves.

I was born as you were born arms wide wide.
They did not baptise me at birth but tried to drown me.
I was born as you were born; naked to the world.
But when they raised me they did not slap me to breathe,
They slapped me to hurt me – they did – to hurt me.
And then, when it was quiet, they slapped me again.
Shock ran through me, through my inside, like electric fire;
Inside, where my blood is. Shock. Shock . . .
And my veins went tight like reins up my arms and up my legs,
Tight and from my head through my chest and to my heart.
They reined in my heart – pulled it tight. Tight.

Then my veins burst out of my body. My veins run away
        from me,
Screaming from my head, running for life, racing from my arms.
My blood, lines. And I do not cry but my eyes wide burn.
        Burn.
And everyone says I have a beautiful smile, but I think my
        smile is not.
Beautifully they beat me when I smile. They said that it was
        the Lord's way.
Then took my smile away. So I runs away. I picks up and
        runs away.

Until the sound of the policeman says, 'What is your name?'
'Your name?' and I say nothing. I say nothing. I am speechless.
        Ma'am . . .
My words have run away, from me. They are hiding somewhere.
And I am turning. I am turning because I am looking for words
And the policeman holds out his hand and I groan and I kick
And I breathe for the first time and all anger is here now
And I scream and scream and scream and they stand back
And they look at my body and they see my bruises
And they say, 'Oh, my God . . . Look at that.'
Like I was a punching bag or something.
And they take me to Care and I call people Staff now.
The shock is in me. Waiting.

In your speech I hear your silence like mine.
Your silence speaks an ocean. I am a girl in a boat

With no oars to row, speaking to you who rule the waves.
Indeed, a child in need. The shock is in me. Waiting, ma'am.

THE QUEEN:

I was born as you were born
And my family torn
And like yours my heart ripped
As blood dripped
And dropped through our generations.

NASEEM MALIK:

No, I was born as you were born,
Naked to the world as you were naked to the world,
Clothed in possibility as you were clothed in possibilities,
Washed in expectation as you were washed in expectation.
Draped in my lineage as you were draped in your lineage!
This is my nation as it is your nation as it is *our* nation.
I had an arranged marriage as *you* had an arranged marriage.
And I wear a veil as you wear the veil.
I speak in tongues alien to your people as you speak in a
           tongue alien to me.

The other day I was serving a man who was taking my service
And he said to me this man, 'Why don't you go back home?',
And I responded as you may have responded;
'This *is* my home,' I said, as you might have said too.

'Dirty immigrant,' he said to me as they have said the same
      to you.
Ninety days Idi Amin gave us, ninety days to leave in 1972.
Where else would we go but back to the . . . motherland
      . . . to you?
To your ninety days.
We came in waves, tired tides of us. We came in waves
And we set up shop and we served your people
As your people, in the same way that your people serve you.

THE QUEEN:

And this country is all the better for your presence
And all the resentment, all the anger thrown at us,
All the spit and the bile and the hatred is not yours,
As you know it is not ours, as you know.

NASEEM MALIK:

I have arrived into myself as you have arrived into yourself.
But I know this, I will protect my children with a vengeance.
No country, no leader, no government will harm them –
You have said this too, haven't you? Understand?

For I was born as you were born,
Washed in expectations as you were washed in expectations.
I like you was born to bloom, my roots pass through poisoned
      earth

Down to fertile soil. They take root, draw nutrients from below
And distribute nutrients above – Love!
This soil is for ever, for ever mine.
I stand before you, as the many before, in line,
To say, I am Muslim, I am British, and I am fine.

THE QUEEN:

I was born as you were born;
Corrupting earthquakes have split our family.
Some have fallen down ravines and I hold their echoes in
          my heart.
On each and every single day that you see me, I hold those
          echoes in.
I was born as you were born. This much is true.
And should I give whispers of wishes rather than speeches,
As I did for my children before they slept,
Then I wish there were no boundaries that all peoples pass
Into one another's houses and all houses are one another's.

RABBI HATTENSTONE:

One another? I am born the same year you are born – 1926.
And so much has happened and yet, so little – Fiddlesticks!
I am an immigrant. I shall always be an immigrant.
I walk like an immigrant. I talk like an immigrant.
I am an immigrant from my tip to my toe.

This word *Immigrant*, you know how it was born?
It emerged from the word *Migrate*. Migrate,
First prescribed as a description of what birds do.
And how free are they? I am an immigrant like the birds.

See. A boy said to me that his zaidy said to him,
Reach for the top of the tree and you get to the first branch.
But reach for the stars and you get to the top of the tree.
So, here is Britain, this beautiful earth, and here is the sky
And here are the stars.

What if for one moment in one day we *reach* for stars?
What if you uncurl your heart as we uncurl ours
And spread your arms open wide as we spread ours?
What if for one moment in one time on one day
We reach out to all and beyond and say,
With the power to draw in the warmth of the sun,
Let it be. Let them come. Let it be. Let them come.

Let them come with their baklava, their coffee and teas.
Like Moses let us lead. Let us all lead.
Let them bring their hymns and their prayer beads.
Let them wear the saints in gold around their necks.
Let them bring their grief and their good, their kismet.
Let them bring their stories and their laughter.
Speak of Christmas and Ramadan and Hanukkah.
Let them ring their church bells, let the muezzin call.

Let the cacophony ring true and ring through to us all.
Let it be. Let them come. Let it be. Let them come.

Let them throw down their seeds and let freedom flower.
Let them speak their own language as we speak ours,
So that we might learn the language of tone and trust,
The blessed language of the body and the face – the language
       of us.
The language of listening. Because these things speak more
Than the clumsiness of words. Let them come. I implore,
Let us exchange our customs and let it be customary to
       exchange.
Let them come like the beautiful life-giving rain.
I shall wear the yarmulke, they shall wear the cloth.
I shall wear the talit, let them wear the cross.
From the churches, the mosques, the synagogues,
Let them come in the name of their gods.

Let them come. It is you that visited them. You.
For whom the sun would never set.
Let us decolonise our minds: Live free, yet, never forget.
You who scoured the world (for who?) like a dragnet
       plunging
Into the waves catching all and sundry lunging into slaves.
It was you who counted the bounty and threw the rest over
       board.
Ruling the waves *indeed* by gun by God by sword.

These British cities thrive today on the cash flow from then.
Then let's address the current, the strong strong current, then.
Lest we stand, as we are, with hands frozen to the gun
On the beaches, in this code red autumnal sun:
Like a kingdom stunned.
Let the knots of history come undone.

Lest we stand, as we are, with hands frozen to the gun
On the beaches, in this code red autumnal sun:
Like a kingdom stunned.
Let the knots of history come undone.
Let your people finish what your people begun.
Let us open our arms as they did – Let them come.

SUMMER OF LOVE: A YEAR IN BLACK AND WHITE

I was born in Billinge, Wigan, in 1967. My mother flew from Addis Ababa, the capital of Ethiopia, to study here. She sought out a social worker who would help with short-term fostering while she finished her studies. I remained in foster care for eleven turbulent years. Apparently I had the devil inside me. The foster parents were Baptists. A revived Christianity was doing a roaring trade in 1967.

From the age of eleven to eighteen, I was harboured in various children's homes in Lancashire. At eighteen, the government (no longer my parent, my legal guardian) left me with a birth certificate and a letter. The birth certificate dated 21 May 1967 revealed my real name: Lemn Sissay. The letter, rifled from my files by a sympathetic social worker, dated 1968, was from my birth mother. 'How can I get Lemn back?' she said. 'I want him to be with his own people, in his own country. I don't want him to face discrimination.'

Like Cool Britannia, the Summer of Love is a marketing invention for a wilting nation and fact for very few. In the following spring of 1968 a master of oratory, Martin Luther King, is shot dead in the US. Within days of this event another master of oratory, Enoch Powell, delivers what becomes known in the UK as the 'Rivers of Blood' speech. These flashes of electricity were the result of the racially charged power surges of 1967. Summer of love for some, summer of hate for many.

Popular culture here in England was swinging its way from party to party with flowers in its hair, a style personified in The Monkees but perfected by The Beatles and relived in *Austin Powers*. Meanwhile *Guess Who's Coming to Dinner?* and *In the Heat of the Night* got a great reception in the US and applause from the UK. Race was the subject of the day, like never before nor since. 'Say it loud,' yelped Mr James Brown in '68. 'I'm black and I'm proud.'

The Black Panther Party arrived in the public consciousness in May 1967. The whole use of the word 'black' to describe people was a new thing. Black was a new thing, black consciousness. Not negro, not nigger, not half-breed or quarter-caste, but black. This raising of consciousness was as relevant to white people as it was to black. The words 'black' and 'white' were never as potent in the twentieth century as in these particular times.

Planet of the Apes was made in the Summer of Love and released the following year. Maybe the British were all too stoned to see what *Planet of the Apes* was really about. The message of the film was not lost on any black person: 'See, if the apes and monkeys get power they'll only do the same, but worse.' Meanwhile Africans were emerging from the calamitous notion of colonialism on to the shores of the motherland. The Anglo-English, sensing the receding hairline of their horizons, clasped their hands to their heads in panic. *Till Death Us Do Part* began on television in 1966. Race is a defining factor of culture in the Sixties, not a peripheral interruption.

However, the children of the post-war coital explosion would wake from their LSD trips entering adulthood in the Seventies fresh-faced and ready to go to work on telling each other and us what a wild time it was and 'If you could remember the Sixties, you really weren't there!' How the Sixties swung, from indifference to indifference, back and forth like some crazed hippy caught in a trip in the centre of the battlefield, curling his fingers to the music and pushing his hands out to shoo bad vibes away. 'Give peace a chance, man, give peace a chance.'

It was a wonderful time for poetry, though. The first book of poetry I received in adolescence was *The Mersey Sound*, published in 1967. I judge all proclamations of poetry's popularity against this year. In Harlem, in what is now known as Marcus Garvey Park, a speech was given by a young guy called Malcolm X but before him were four men reading poetry to a drum beat – The Last Poets – the Godfathers of the most popular form of performed literature in the twentieth century, rap. And, as if passing on the baton from one age of African-American poetry to another, in 1967 the poet laureate of Harlem and the Harlem Renaissance, Langston Hughes, passed away.

But if you were white in England you had choices, you liked The Beatles or The Stones – how revolutionary a choice is that? That the hippy 'ideal' was anything more than the emotionally illiterate and politically naïve choosing to ignore the obvious changes in society with general platitudes, is anathema to the facts. In 1969 The Rolling Stones hired Hells Angels to do the security at their gig. The Hells Angels hated black people and were virtual white supremacists.

What does this say, not about the Hells Angels but about The Rolling Stones and their generation? This performance went down in rock 'n' roll history and was filmed. The security stabbed a man to death at the gig, a black man. The concert continued. It's the perfect metaphor for the Sixties attitude to black people. It was a summer of love for those who preached innocence and played ignorance. Make way for the stretcher so we can party on. History gathers no moss like a rolling stone.

So, when I hear of Oasis or Weller, and the great Beatles influence, when I hear of young up-and-coming artists harking back to The Beatles in some kind of retro chic way, I remember not what they produced in this enlightened summer, but the misinformation of the time and how black people, like Indians, were either demonised or hero-worshipped but god forbid they would be accepted as neighbours. I was that neighbour.

The process of colonialism was ending, Britannia no longer ruled the waves, and the British were realising how small these islands really were, and they were shocked and angry. A new Africa awoke, led by Ethiopia and its emperor, Haile Selassie, who was in England at the time and the first African king to speak at the United Nations.

In the midst of this, my mother left Ethiopia to visit this country to study in Oxfordshire. The following year, as

Martin Luther King died in a river of blood, as the world mourned, as Enoch Powell incited race hatred in his apocalyptic speech, The Beatles released The Beatles album which, firstly in America, was unofficially named *The White Album*. The cover design was entirely white. The word 'black' has never been more associated with race and by proxy the word 'white'.

Fran Landesman, an elfin Jewish New York poet, performed to electrified audiences in London throughout the sixties. She would take her place on the stage, the guitarist would punch out a few chords as she released the poem, 'White Nightmare'. I was born into this.

ACKNOWLEDGEMENTS

Grateful acknowledgements go to the *Guardian* newspaper for publishing 'Summer of Love: A Year in Black and White'. To BBC Radio Four for commissioning 'The Queen's Speech' as part of its *From Fact to Fiction* series. 'The Boxer' was written for Phil Martin's family and broadcast on BBC Television's sports programme *On the Line*. 'Winter: Shepherd's Warning', 'Spring: Mayday Mayday', 'Summer: Mountain Top' and 'Autumn: Lost Bronze' were commissioned by the International Society of Contemporary Music and made into an album *Words and Pictures* with Apollo Sax Quartet. 'Red Sky Dawn', 'Transistor', 'Dei Miracole', 'Doris' and 'Elephant in the Room' were all commissioned by BBC Radio Four's *Saturday Live*. 'Catching Numbers' was commissioned by GMPTE and can be seen inside Manchester's Shudehill Station. 'Horizons' was commissioned by Northwest Regional Development Agency.

'The Gilt of Cain' is written into a sculpture in Fen Court in the City of London. It was a Futurecity commission on behalf of the City of London. 'Rain' was commissioned by Manchester City Council and can be seen upon the wall on Dilworth Street, Manchester. 'The Battle of Adwa, 1896' was commissioned by Daniel Truneh of the Ethiopian embassy. 'Olympic Invocation' was written for and published in *New Departures*, edited by Michael Horovitz. 'Flags' was commissioned by The Northern Quarter in Manchester and is inlaid upon the flagstones of Tib Street. 'The Man in the Hospital' was commissioned by Gordon House, head of BBC Drama at the World Service. On World AIDS Day 'The Man in the Hospital' was performed and broadcast on the World Service from Mermaid Theatre, London. 'Manchester Piccadilly' was commissioned by Argent.

'Listener' was commissioned by Gordon House then read and broadcast at the seventieth birthday celebrations of the BBC World Service. 'The Actor's Voice' was also a Gordon House BBC commission. 'Perfect' was broadcast on a BBC Radio Four documentary produced by Philip Sellars, about the film of the night train which included the W.H. Auden poem *Night Mail*.

I would like to thank Jude Kelly of the Southbank Centre and The Paul Hamlyn Foundation. If it had not been for the Southbank Centre's support and residency, *Listener* would not be here now. I would like to thank Gill Lloyd of Artsadmin. Grateful acknowledgements go to Hannah Azieb Pool for her kindness and patience. Thank you Jamie Byng, Francis Bickmore and the entire Canongate team.